THE DESPONDENT

© Copyright Aaron Stone 2020 - All rights reserved. The resale or reproduction of this book either partially or in its entirety is strictly forbidden.

Illustrations © Renae Stone 2020 - All rights reserved. Used with permission.

The Despondent
First Edition 2020

Paperback ISBN: 978-0-6489461-0-6
ePub ISBN: 978-0-6489461-1-3
Mobipocket ISBN: 978-0-6489461-2-0

Disclaimer: Anything written in this book comes from the authors personal perspective at time of initial writing. The author is by no means a qualified anything, and as such, nothing should be taken as advice (legal, medical, psychiatrical or otherwise). Contents herein may be of graphic nature, and may bring back some awful memories and mental states of those whom have suffered, are suffering, or know someone who has had depression or suicidal tendencies. This book is compiled to help those suffering to understand they aren't alone; and for those who know someone who is suffering, or who has passed by suicide, some things which may be going on inside such a person with these mental illnesses. A lot of the poetry and short stories were written by the author whom was suffering (and diagnosed with) Major Depression Disorder at the time of original writing before print. If you or someone you know is suffering depression, anxiety, PTSD, any other mental illness or are experiencing suicidal thoughts, please reach out to someone you can trust – teacher, friend, pastor, doctor. You are not alone in this fight. You can win this, even though you might not be feeling like you can at this particular time.

To all our children,
Never let anyone tell you that you aren't good enough.
If you have a goal, a dream, an idea – run with it!
You are worthy, you are beautiful, you are capable, you are loved.

This book is dedicated to those we have lost
and to those whom are still fighting the internal war.
It can be won.
You can win.
You aren't alone.

Aleysha, you are forever in our hearts,
Always loved and never forgotten.

"Oh! To be writing again.'
These words echo through my mind.
'What should you write about? Of what should you pen?'
Nothing comes to mind.
'Perhaps a beetle with it's hard shell and small size?'
No, I need something deeper.
My mind retraces it's steps:
Love.
Hatred.
Despair.
'What about 'hope'?'
Well, what about it? I knew it once. I don't remember it now, though.
My mind idles once again - unsure of where to go.
'Nothing is certain in this world.'
Yes, I know that.
'So, take a step in blind faith?'
Faith? I'm pretty certain I have lost all faith.
'"Nothing is certain," remember?'
Smart arse.
'So what to write about?'
I glance up at the page in front of me. A story unfolding?
'All you need is a collection of thoughts.'
Yes.
'So what will you write about?'
I don't answer.
I have no answer.
I am alone with my thoughts - penning them to paper.
'The world will one day see.'
See what?
'Your thoughts. They're an open book now.'

Yes, they are.
'Aren't you...?'
I am.
I can't stop though.
I must write until my pen stops.

It has stopped. For now.

'The pen never stops. For as long as you breathe, you are observing, and have something to write.'

This is true. I hate how my mind operates, sometimes.
'I know. It's for your own good, though.'
How?
'In time... In time you shall see.'
Ah, the "Waiting Game" again.
'Yes. You will one day learn patience, as well.'
I roll my eyes and glance out the window.
'The sky is blue today.'
No shit?
'It's also quite hot.'
Why do you think I'm inside?
No response.
Score one for me.
A few minutes pass, then:
'There is a moral - a point - to this.'
I know. I can't put it to words, though.
'That's okay. Those reading it will understand.'
Perhaps. I doubt it though. I'll never be good enough to be understood.
'They will. Each will interpret this differently for themselves.'
True.
'...and don't speak like that. You're amazing'
Liar. I'm pathetic.
'You aren't. I'm not."

The Finish Line:

Generally, when someone has depression or anxiety, we will self-isolate. We will withdraw. We won't seek help. Why should we? No one cares about us anyway, right? And the more we start to think like this, the more we believe it, and further into the darkness we are drawn.

This darkness can eventually become our safe-haven. A place where no one can reach us, touch us, hurt us. It is nothing but ourselves here. As cold, isolated and lonely this place is, we are warm. We are welcome. We are familiar. We are safe.

And on this path of self-destruction we continue.

Quite often (And I'd wager more often than not), we don't see this as self-destruction. We are still alive and breathing, right? We survived our last attempt, and besides, we are only in this place because someone else did something to trigger us and put us in this dark hole to begin with.

As Bob Ezrin and Roger Waters of Pink Floyd write in their song '*The Trial*', "There must have been a door there in the wall when I came in." There wasn't ever a door, because we build the walls up ourselves around us, one dirty brick at a time of self-loathing, fear, anxiety, depression, regret...

And what does trigger the anxiety or depression within us? For some, it's a scent. Others, a song or sound. Someone yelling at their disruptive child in the shopping centre. A conversation we're currently having, which started off with us happy, only to suddenly be reminded of ONE thing, completely unintended by anyone participating in the conversation (or even unrelated), and BAM! it's all downhill for an hour or five...

Why don't we reach out? Well, sometimes we do. However, quite often it is said we are "looking for attention" (and this may be true, though perhaps not how it is meant by the person stating it), or it's done in the most subtlest of ways for fear of further rejection.

    I remember Mum recognised my depression when I was 18. She, our neighbour, and my step-dad, sat me down to talk to me and I threw it in their face. I don't think I said anything, so when I did eventually open my mouth, I would have only yelled and swore at them, stormed off to my room. (This, among other things, eventually lead to my mother kicking me from the house, rendering me homeless for the first time). All I could do was to drown out all the thoughts and pain their prodding arose with the loudest, angriest music I could find. That, for me, was a healthy escape. Others might think that listening to songs like Pantera's "Fucking Hostile", Marilyn Manson's "The Fight Song", and Slipknot's "Everything Ends" might not be a good idea because of my current headspace, but for me, these musicians knew how I was feeling, so I could relate to them and connect and vent and get it all out. It was the therapy I needed at the time.

    We are broken and crying inside, but our exterior could be smiling and laughing because we don't want people to know that something is wrong. If someone thinks something is wrong, then they'll likely suggest therapy and medication, (or worse, *pity* us); and quite frankly, the idea of this scares the hell out of us. I remember I saw a therapist once, and she sent me home because I was in a good mood and didn't want to ruin a happy day for me by making me delve into my past and issues. That obviously wasn't too helpful. I said to myself that I may as well not turn up ever because all I must have to do is stay smiling and happy and suck it up. It took me two years to start seeing someone again. I went to maybe five sessions. The therapist said something I didn't like and I never saw another one again for another six years or so, which came about after a separation between me and the mother of my child. The best kind of therapist I've found so far personally? Poetry, the ocean, and personal development books. If traditional therapy isn't something you're ready to try, there will be another way which may work for you in the meantime.

And sometimes, traditional therapy mediums aren't always the answer to help at all. Regardless of the method you choose to take, something has to happen inside us. I found therapy to be like a school teacher – there to help, but not really there to give us the answer. We work out the answers ourselves through a lot of blood, sweat, and tears; but we can't do it alone. We need people around us to patiently hold out their hand, waiting for us to ask for help. It has to be our decision, not yours.

THERE IS NO QUICK FIX.

I know people won't agree with me on most of this, but that's how it was for me, and that's all I can write about. Everyone is different. Everyone copes and deals with things differently. For me, I didn't deal with anything for the longest of times. Shoved it down, bottled it up. I was angry. I had the right to be angry. Everyone should be allowed to get angry at some point. It's very unhealthy to keep frustrations bottled up inside. The difference, I suppose, is the way we channel our anger, our sadness, our depression, anxiety, et cetera. Find a healthy way – running, reading, writing poetry... Anything that releases you from your chains.

"It's okay to be not okay" is only partially correct. If you're not okay, that's okay, but don't hold it in and pretend to be strong and able to carry your burdens. My Mum did that for decades only to attempt suicide a week after my 30th birthday. Always thought she was the one with her head screwed on and strong and able. It eventually got too much for her. Thankfully, she is still with us today, but the message is there in black and white. Carrying it with you without talking to someone will only work for so long. For some of us it's months or a few years, others, it could take decades. Eventually, it may get too much for us as we all have our breaking points.

If you are struggling and do not know where to turn, here in Australia we are lucky to have many organisations which are there to support people like me, like my mum, my sisters, my friends, and you. Speak to your GP and they will direct you to the right people to talk to. Call one of the many mental health helplines available.

Talk, cry, don't talk, don't cry. It's up to you...

BUT REMEMBER YOU ARE NOT ALONE.

THE DESPONDENT
Part One

The Poetry

The poems reflect where my thoughts, feelings, and truths once lay during the darkest spots of my depression.

I hope they can reflect the seriousness of depression and how hopeless one feels when suffering this illness.

I hope they can help those suffering know that they aren't alone in this fight.

The experiences depicted in these are real.

I felt and believed these to be true in complete explicit detail.

A Sense Of Self

In the depths of the darkest of nights,
Whom will you call to save you from your demons?
God abandoned you,
You dishonoured your family,
No one wants a rotten apple.
Screaming into the cold, empty abyss
You think you hear someone reply.
You stupid wretch
It is your own echo.
Dance around your own soul
Torture your broken body more
Laugh loud and proud at your decaying flesh
Satan is coming for you now.

Where Is Love?

Angels are falling
Dropping from the heavens
Their screams fill the night
Like a tortured being in the pits of hell

Where is love if not where they came?
It is forsaken in these lands
The night surrounds me
Darkness covers me
Like a blanket of coldness and hate

In Another Life

In another life
Nothing is the same
Spirits have a name
Life is a dream

In another life
Distance is not an issue
Spirits can roam freely
Humanity can't destroy

In another life
Life is wanted
Happiness consumes
Darkness has no grounds

In another life...

As The Rain Falls Down

On this stormy night
The rain pours down
And the sky doth the lightning light
I feel so alone
All I want is her arms
And her comfort that might
Still be there
My cigarette burns
Away at my lungs
Taking my breath
As her love once did
But here I sit alone
Feeling empty this night
Hearing only the thunder
As the rain falls down tonight

My Eyes Awaken

boom.
        cut.
                hang.
                        sink.
                                fly.
                                        fall.
                                                sleep.

Which will be my exit?
When will I find that door?
All alone with people around.
I dont exist within a crowd.
With ties that bind;
These ropes pull tight suffocating me in the night.
I see these rhymes and i cant decide which i hate most:
The words that flow
Or this life I know.

Would someone cut me?
Drown me?
Take me to my death?

Can I, like Icarus,
Make wings and fly,
Touch the sun
And fall and die?

Or maybe swim to only sink
And sleep eternally in the cold darkness
To be eaten by fish?

Is there anybody there
Who can grant me my wish?

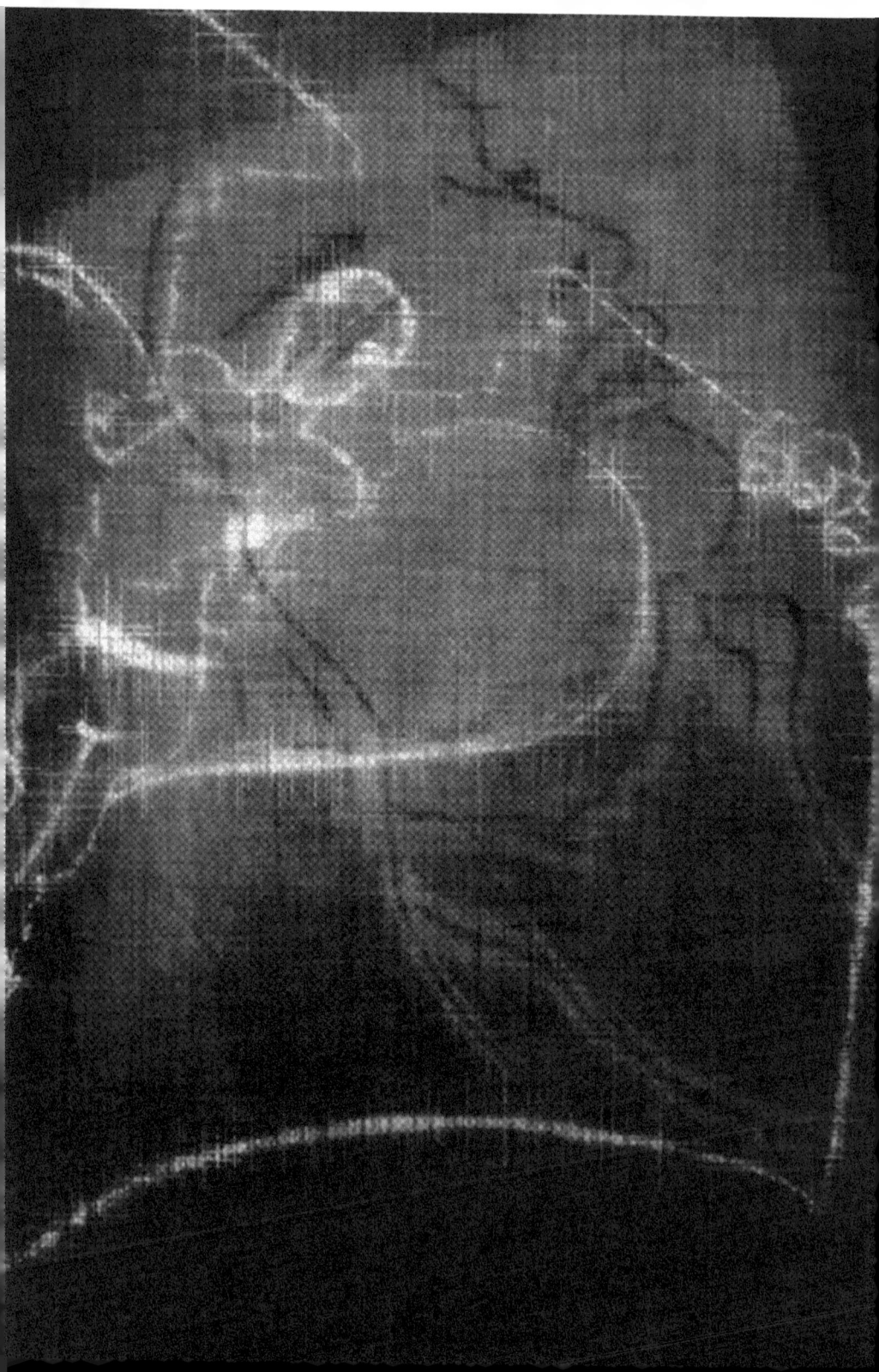

Untitled

Disappearing into thin air
Near invisible like cigarette smoke
My presence will always linger here
Even after another half a year
New year, new life
New promises, new lies

Betrayal and pain will always appear
No matter how great the distance is
But we'll get by and we'll be fine
New day, new life
New man, you're his next wife
And my pain will always be there

Hanging above my head Like a ceiling fan
City lights and city fights
Lightning strikes, there goes another life
But tomorrow is a new day
And tomorrow you'll find another way
To throw sticks and throw stones
To find a new way to shut me down

But I'm always going to be here
You got me through to see another year
In the distance, in the shadows
You were my greatest cheer

I never knew how much I hurt you though
A day came and we ceased to speak
We only fought and dirtied sheets
Still I never knew how much I hurt you

But today I'm going to see it through
Tomorrow is another day
Into the distance you'll try to make me fade
A broken memory and a broken home
Is all I'll end up being to you.

The Birthplace of Hatred

I want to slit your wrists
Choke you, gut you
Bleed you out
Nothing less can come of this
Fucking die, you fat fuck

All these fucking years
Drowning your kids with your religious dogma
Did you ever believe it for yourself?
That God you claim to worship
Has a special place in Hell for
Cunts Like You

You're a fucking animal
Can I take you to the slaughterhouse
You're halfway there
Rotting in your cell
Will someone give me the keys?
I'm coming in for the kill!

RIP
STAB
SLASH

And through your screams and
Tears of anguish
I give you a taste of Hell
As I laugh loudly,
Covered in your blood,
I'm coming in for the Kill!

The Prisoner Within.

White knuckled,
I grip the icy cold steel bars surrounding me;
My screams barely heard by my captors
As I rattle my cage
Wanting to break free.
The guards torment me,
laughing and spitting in my face.
Cutting me down with words
Sharper than any double-edged sword.

Doubts. Fears. Lies. Betrayal. Hatred.

Scars of my past cover my body
Like deep, bleeding wounds.
The names and faces associated with them
Are the chains binding me to the harsh, rocky ground.
I start to give in to it all;
Wondering if it's worth my energy...

A Prisoner Of Me

FUCK YOU
There's **NOTHING LEFT**
You can take from me

    But you keep pulling
        Yes you keep taking
Until my skin is bone
        Get   off   your   throne!

    Once you have gone
        I'll have
            NOTHING LEFT
      You'll have **take**n away
My   **everything**

    When **nothing** is
            left
      I'll be alone
And won't
        go home

Because **I** will **have**
      no   home

    GET THE FUCK
AWAY   FROM   ME

    Taking everything
        Is nothing new for me

      GET   THE   FUCK
    AWAY   FROM   ME

  Because   **there's**   nothing   left

      I **can't**
b r e a k   free
        From
    Me

Morbidity

The cold icy steel of the screwdriver
Rolls across your palm as you play with it in your mind.
Such a sweet sensation -
A beautiful release of all the hate, anger and pain -
It would be easy to drive it through your wrist
And tear it across towards your body
Through your arm,
Shattering bone, tormenting muscle,
Tearing ligaments and tendons.
Create a cut that never heals...
Much like the one that is your heart.
A smile paints your face and
Brightens the dark room in which you sit
As you remember what brought you here.
The realisation that you were right.
You were right all along,
And the rest of those bastards are full of shit.
You were right.
Everything -
Life, thought, beauty, love -
Is a freakin' dream-zone
From which no one can be pulled from.
Standing the screw driver upon its tip
On your own fingers
You see the face of death smiling,
Welcoming you to join its parade,
In its vial reflection;
And you laugh one last time as you flip
The screwdriver around, holding it tightly in your fist,
And drive it through your temple.
You feel the warm, smooth flow of blood
Slowly run over your hand and down the side
Of your face as you fall to your knees whispering
"Goodbye."

Die In Misery

A rusty cage
A broken name
A hated face
A burned down town
Infected race
Horrific dream

Life!
It's no fairy tale
What you see is what you get
Now play the hand
You have been dealt

A rusty cage
A broken name
A hated face
A burned down town
Infected race
Horrific dream

All around you
Darkness falls
Never to be a new dawn
So face the world
Spit in it's face
Or die in misery

Now die in misery
Now die in misery
Face your fate
Or rot in this place
And die in misery

...Or is this an horrific dream??

The Unknown Embodies The Invisible

As I stand and watch your tears bleed from your eyes,
I cannot help but smile.
The way your eyes are shining,
And tears streaming down your face,
Make me think of a warm spring day
Overlooking a gentle waterfall from a grassy meadow
Somewhere in this harsh world -

Somewhere where pain, and destruction,
Have not yet corrupted,
And where beauty lingers on.

The beauty of pain and suffering.
The joy of seeing people cry in anguish
And hearing them scream in terror is like a soothing lullaby
A mother would sing her newborn child.

It takes me places,
Like a dream of fond memories and brutal instruments of death.
I laugh in wonder as I observe what is surrounding me -
Nothing but peace and solitude.
The murderous torture in my mind quietens.
Yet I can still feel the pain of the departed
And the guilt of those left behind.

Anger. Fear.

This whole place stinks of it.
No one wants to know, think, dream.
Yet all suffer from what they see.
Blood dripping off the wooden benches
Onto the cold stone floor below, slowly flowing -
Like a creek in the bush when the tide is on its way in -
To the corner of this god-forsaken room.

In The Midst Of Everything

Staring into these burning embers
I feel my soul evaporating into the darkness.
My only light is that coming from the flames of this hell.
The warmth is... subtle beauty.
All I can do is hide away so that I can't be seen.
Eyes everywhere searching,
Trying to find the real me.
Whispers echo through me asking me who I am.
Movement in the distance.
It's time for me to go before someone gets too close.
I don't want to be found or known.
The heat is excruciating yet somehow I am so cold.
Where am I?
Suddenly I don't know what is real.

Hinges

Time passes slowly in this dark place
Time passes slowly for those who wait
The darkness comes and times slows down
What are we waiting for? Why do we wear frowns?
Silence drags on and silence lingers
For nothing we bear can take of the hinges
The hinges of hate, love and faith
The hinges of the door that shows our true fate

A Life Without

Time slides slowly by and nothing seems to change
There's no peace
Nothing to bring solitude to those living in fear and sorrow
There's no heaven that i can enter
No hell that isn't earth that won't accept me
Darkness consumes and steals away the light of our love
Here i am a million miles away and nothing makes sense
There is no exit,
No avenue that either of us can take
There is nothing,
No path that will lead us to escape
The pain and evil that haunts us with every step we make

Unfold Your Sorrows

Unfold your sorrows
Scream into the darkness
Let your bloody tears
Colour your cheeks
And have your voice fill the night

Throw yourself into a wall
Bust your knuckles against its harsh frame
Finish another bottle! That's right.
And run naked in the rain

Tear at your hair
Rip at your skin
Destroy the filthy shell you live in

Fuck yourself
Fuck your life
And let your empty remains rot
On the muddy ground I spit upon

A HORROR STORY

The darkness swallows me.
Life is great when it's only me.
Only me and my thoughts to keep me company.
Thoughts of horror, and my wrists bleeding.
Psychopaths smiling and laughing in the face of their victims,
Screaming: "Bleed bitch, bleed! Fucking bleed!"

Can you feel their pain when you watch that shit?
Can you relate? Does it take you back
To when you were a kid, when your father
Always beat on you and your mother?
Feels good, don't it?
Makes you feel warm and invincible inside, hey?

There's nobody but the darkness accompanied by your thoughts
On a cold and stormy night when the girl on The Exorcist
Fucks herself deep
With that bloody and mangled crucifix.
Do you feel sorry for her? Or do you laugh manically
and enjoy the brutality playing in front of you?

Sometimes it feels like it isn't only me here.
Sometimes I can hear the dead walking these halls
and I can feel them touch me on the shoulder and peer
into this glowing screen on which I write.
Does it make me warm and comfortable,
Or is something going to jump out and slice me?

Jesus won't save me if I grip the cross tight.
Jesus isn't here. He died long ago.
And if he isn't here to save me,
Then nothing will.
So I sit back and watch demons climb out of the TV
To tear me up and torment me.

Between the Lines of Death and Life

Close my eyes
Fall asleep
Leave this place
In darkness deep

I dont want to live
I want to see
Take my life
And set me free

I can't survive
This darkness binds
My soul parts my body
I am no longer blind

Open your minds
By closing your eyes
Can you see what is beyond?
There are no more lies

Freedom lives on
My body rots in the ground
I was lost in life
And in death I am found

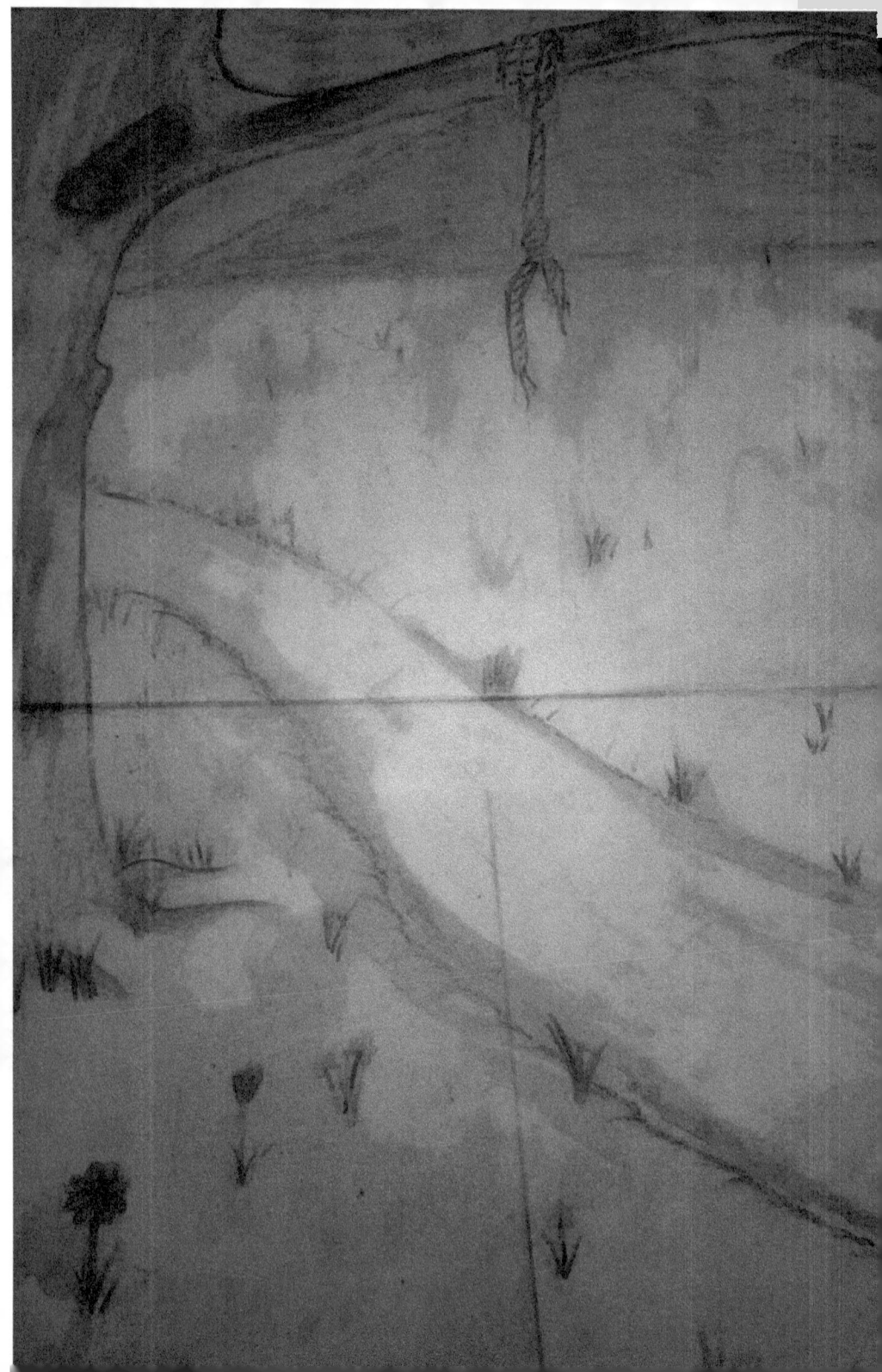

What Happened To You?

The refreshing rain falls.
The cold night passes.
The soothing music plays.
What happened to you?

The warm sun shines.
The beach brings joy.
Cars pass us by,
But what happened to you?

You used to always laugh.
You used to always smile.
You used to bring us fun.
So what happened to you?

Something in you snapped.
Something in you clicked.
Something around you broke.
Now you are no more.

Shadows Of A Forsaken World

The past is behind and
Herein lays the future
Hid in darkness and unbeknown
To even the wisest amongst us

If we open our eyes and our hearts
We can move forward without fear

Holding onto the truth
It will light our way and
Guide us through our doubts

Open the doors and
Let the light shine on through
And there will be rejoicing once again
In the shadows of a forsaken world.

Betrayal

My demons from my past are resurfacing
Hostile like a wild lion being prodded in a tormented cage
One more jab is all it will take to break my demons free
Controlling me
Dangerously
And into the night I'll be gone forever
No longer seen

I fucking hate myself
God and the devil could do anything now
It won't change a thing
Because hating ones self
Could be my greatest sin

So fuck you
And fuck me please
I'm broken, trapped
Soon to be free
My demons closing in on me

Nothing can be done to save me now
Forgiveness in the wind

Chased Away

When required for a while and then we can disappear for now.
The little things set us free.
Who can make the sun go down and who knows when the dawn will break.
Forever is never - for time is forgotten
Fasten your mind before you leave this time.
In regards to everything,
Regarding nothing at all:
May your blessings be upon you and ever shall they grow.

Ever shall the path be lit that your feet doth follow -
To whom this may concern, and to whose concern grows curious,
Do not think for one second.
Only be. Simply drift.
Tomorrow morning shall never come again.
Live today, it is your end.
When you wake, you will suffocate
When you dream you will die;
But whilst you breathe, discover that life is a mind-f**k ride.
To end this now, feel robbed.
Be broken.

Remember this is my story...

A lullaby was once rewritten to entice a nightmare.
Happy dreams and solemn fears.
Murky these rivers run
Halloween. Hallows eve.
Dawn comes.
The dead grow frightened.
We never can know someone.
Only what they want you to see
No one will know the real you.
Hiding inside, you are broken - let go.
Be free.

Will life be likely to make sense?
Will you find your present tense?
Can the rocks create the wind by knocking down some trees?
Forever in a sense of dismay.
Finding humour where it lays
A twisted and tormented rose is threatened by its very own vines.
Cultured and cured now like the rest
Have you your own ideas?
No way! Put them to rest!

This tale ends with a full moon,
Shining brightly behind a cloud.
Much light. Many colours.
Screaming to be seen.
The rivers might flow at peace again.
Clear how they had always been.

THE DESPONDENT
Part Two

The Short Stories

*I wrote these during my darkest times,
as I did the poetry you have
already read in this book.*

*Let them serve as a metaphor
describing the internal torment,
confusion,
void,
turmoil*

The experiences depicted in these are real.

I felt like this in complete explicit detail.

A LOST SOUL

"Where am I? What is this place?"
He looks around.
The streets are dark. They're cold.
He hears a voice.
Is it his own?
He looks up into the street light towering above him.
He moves forward out of its glare one step at a time.
He's scared.
Alone.
He does not know this place. He does not know the time. The year.
He's afraid.
Another noise.
To his right, he thinks.
He spins around, searching frantically for the source.
He calls out.
There's no response.
He calls louder: "Hey! Is there anybody out there?"
Still no response.

He moves his hand onto his forehead and wipes the cold sweat aside, drying his hand on his tattered jumper that barely is enough to ward off the winter chill. He drops to his knees in the filthy snow and draws an arrow pointing forwards.
At the base of the arrow, he draws another one. This one points to his left.
He draws a circle around it.

Standing back up, he begins to stumble his way forwards into the dark. He holds himself, shivering, trying to keep warm.

"Where am I? I don't know this place. I'm lost."

He realises he's asking himself questions.

"Am I answering them myself, too? Have I lost my mind? I don't have a mind. I don't even know who I am. What is this place? Who am I?"

He holds his hands, palms stretched outwards and upwards in front of him. His fingertips peer through the torn ends of his black, worn out, wooly gloves. He brings them to his lips and breathes his cold breath upon them in an attempt to warm his fingers. He sticks his hands in his pockets and continues his aimless stride into the night. Stumbling over hidden rocks and ditches under the shallow snow that covers the cobblestone street, he looks to his left.

A light?
A scream?

He closes his eyes tightly, then reopens them and looks again.
There is nothing.
Only the abandoning silence of the dark night to keep him from losing his wits.

"Losing my wits? What wits? You lost your mind remember.."
"That's right, I did. What? Wait? Who said that?"
"I said that," came the snivelling response out of his own mouth.

Fuck.

I think I've lost it, he thinks to himself.
He screams out again to no avail.

"You're alone. No one cares. No one will hear you no matter how loudly you cry."
"Fucken shut up. Stop it." He kicks the back of his leg and takes a few more steps into the night. "Stop talking. Stop answering yourself. You're fine. In the morning, you'll be fine."
"Ha! What morning? You know this place. You've been here before. There's no denying it."

He stops dead in his tracks and slowly scans his surroundings

through the thick mist and cold darkness. "No."
"Oh yes, indeed. You definitely know this place. It is Dolor[1]."

He shakes his head furiously trying to silence the bastard within. "Go away. I don't know you!"
"Oh, but you do. I've been with you since childhood."

He thrusts his hands against the wall he's been following hard and screams out in pain. He looks at his hands. The gloves have torn some more.
Blood is seeping through.

He stares at the gnarly wall with enough bitterness to destroy a legion of souls and curses it in a mindless rage. He drops to the ground, on his knees, with his hands in fists against the ground in front of him and sobs.

"Why have I come back to this place? Who am I? What did I do?"
He hears jeering and mock-laughter echoing around the walls and through his head. They're shouting his name and hurling insults at him in every tongue known to mankind.
He tears at his face and arms trying to remove the ugliness of flesh from his body. He digs his nails into his cheeks and screams in agony as he feels a chunk of himself tear away.
The blood is warm as it seeps down his face and wrists.

He laughs manically and continues tearing at himself until there is no face left.
He is sitting in a puddle of bloody snow, surrounded by chunks of flesh from his face and forearms.
He screams in pain and accomplishment.

"Here! Are you happy now?" He cries out to no one but the darkness.
"Have I served my purpose?"

---

[1] *Dolor is Latin for pain, grief, misery, suffering*

He pulls himself up so that he's half-standing, half-leaning, against the torturesome wall and smiles at it. "Or shall I pay for more of my sins?"

He screams loudly as he thrusts punch after punch into the wall, ripping chunks of skin, flesh and bits of bone off his hands with each connection.
He takes a step backward to examine his bloody art. He throws his head back, laughing, before crumpling to the ground.
He lay there bleeding himself out onto the filthy, dark, cold ground; and this is where he lay until death take over...

These are the final words, final actions, final thoughts, of a man with no hope left in his life, before he takes the final plunge into madness, and ends his life to find happier days on the other side.

How do I know all this?

The answer is simple:
I'm already dead...
That man...
Was me.

THE STORY OF ANNE

"Fuck off! Go away! Leave me alone!" The young girl shrieked in terror, tears were gushing out of her reddened eyes. "Fucking leave me alone! Do you know what it's like to.. to be stepped on? Crushed. Beaten. Bruised. Left for dead all bloody and broken on the sidewalk? Do you fucking know? Of course not! You don't know fucking shit, Murray!"
She picked herself up off the cold, rocky floor she was sprawled across and tried one more time to claw her way out of her stone chamber, while her captor stood above her laughing.
"Ha! Cry! Bleed! Scream!" His voice was menacing. "Go on! Scream out at the top of your lungs. No one's gonna save you! No one cares about you, ya filthy whore!" He spat down at her as he turned and walked away, leaving her sobbing to herself.
"Anne, what have you gotten yourself into now..." She cried to herself.

Her memories took her back to when she was a child, playing at home on the coast where she lived. She smiled through her tears as she remembered herself running through the back door all muddy from the rain that morning. Her mother was appalled. "Annabel Stacey Bedrinn! What have you gotten into this time?" Young Anne stood there and laughed; "There's worms in the mud, Mummy. Come look..."

The sound of heavy footsteps brought Anne back to reality. She looked up to see a rusty bucket flung down at her and some dried out bread. She rushed to catch it before it hit the ground; but the bucket was too quick for her and smashed against the ground to pieces, the water that was once inside now ran along the dirty ground like a small stream. She scraped with her fingers what water she could make cling to her hands and sucked it from her skin and picked up the bread and took a small nibble after dusting a few flakes of dirt off it.

Her dreams that night were violent and restless, like every other night. The next morning Anne woke up to a sudden bite of high-pressured, freezing cold water. The force was almost enough to break her bones.

A few moments passed before a cold, vicious-looking, rusty chain was thrown down to her, fastened at the top of her chamber, waiting impatiently for her to drag herself up it.

"Come on bitch!" Murray spat down at her. "And no bullshit today, else you'll be tied up with the pigs for the next month."

Anne fought back the pain as she pulled herself up the tormented chain, using her feet to walk up the wall, and trying to avoid tearing her skin apart on the nasty barbs and spikes that had been welded onto it.

Outside, the rain was coming down like a ton of bricks. Thunder and lightning lit up the skies, making the surrounding landscape look frightening, like something that belonged in an horror film.

Anne looked around at what had supposedly become her home over the last few... She struggled to remember yet again how long she had been kept a victim of her malicious ex-boyfriend. Was it months? Years? She turned to her left and trudged through the muddy yard to the beaten shack that would hopefully provide her some shelter from the harsh weather - the same shack that Murray had threatened minutes beforehand to keep her in. The yard was surrounded by a large fence with ten-thousand volts of electricity running through them to keep the animals from running off. Well, that was it's original purpose, Anne thought to herself as she curled up in a dark, smelly corner. She sat there for a while in silence wondering where she went wrong, what she had ever done to deserve a life of imprisonment like this.

"What the fuck did I do to deserve all this?" She screamed, beating her forehead and forearms against the wall.

Photographic images of her Mother and sister laughing and playing flooded her mind, and then the tears came gushing out of her eyes. Nothing she did would stop them from coming. "Better here than where Murray would see," she morbidly thought.

A few hours later, the rain had died down, and Anne woke up to getting violently dragged through the paddock, getting kicked and yelled at all the way back to her chamber. Her broken, wiry frame looked like it had gone through a meat shredder by the time she was being tied and lowered like a cow to a hungry brood of sharks into her cell below. At the bottom, Anne fought the chain from around her stomach and ran to the far corner, hiding from its vicious lashes as Murray thrust it in every direction trying to hit her with it as slowly he wound it back up to his feet.

"You stupid slut! Trying to hide away from me again! You're lucky I don't tie your wrists in the barbed wire next time!" Anne heard him spit in disgust as he slammed a big wooden door behind him on his way out.

The room was black as pitch now, and the only sound to keep herself company that night was the sound of her breathing, as it was for her every night. Was she ever going to be free?

The Diary of a Broken Man

This isn't a story, but is a collection of my thoughts I wrote down back in 2008. Here they are, explicit, raw, unedited, naked for your own understanding into the mind of my 21-year-old self...

Laying here in the lonely cold once again with nothing specific going through my mind.
A funeral scene portrays the silent serenity of death on the TV.
It makes me question the essence of life.
Why are we here? Do we pay notice to those we have around? Or are they only here to fill in a few blank spots in our own meaningless existance?
Our parents tell us to treat others as we want to be treated, but in the reality of it, life doesn't work that way.
Life's what you make of it; but a word of warning is that regardless how nice you try to be, people will always be assholes to you at some point - even parents, friends, everyone. So I lay here wondering why bother? What's the point? Now for a contradiction: My thoughts tell me with all that said, we should still try.
It doesn't make sense. None of anything does make sense.
A christian family, an abusive father - and it's broken. If christianity and all its teachings can't keep a family together, then what can? My theory says it has nothing to do with religion or values. The only thing that can keep a family together is love. Love isn't God, Heaven, or any of that. Love is an emotion enforcing an action. That's what I believe anyway. Maybe it's the other way around? An action enforcing an emotion, perhaps? Who knows? Maybe it goes both ways.
Two hours have passed and not even a page has been writ. That's kind of like my life: 21 years and nothing to show. A half-written story still in development, with the author seated behind the glowing screen of his monitor trying to decide what is to become of his character.
I guess I have ideas. Little hints and clues of what I want out of this

life. I guess all I'm lacking is the support, teachings, and guidance to get me there - where ever "there" may be...

Shit happens in everyones life. Why does it drag me so far down then, and not for others? Is it because my shit differs from theirs? We're all unique, living our own unique existance, but none of us are completely unique. Somewhere out there, someone is going through what we are, or what we have recently come out of, or what we are about to go into. It makes me wonder why someone is able to go through what I have, or worse than, and not even be half affected by it as I am.

I have my good days. A week could pass where nothing goes wrong, and I start questioning myself. I wonder if I am only having myself on. That my depression is another bullshit lie... Then thoughts like that will creep in, reminding me of the lies and pain, embarrassment, hurt, hate and anger that I have gone through - and these thoughts, these memories, bring with them anger and depression. I begin to feel like shit again. I begin to feel at home. I welcome these darknesses. I find comfort and familiarity with it, so I don't want it to leave. It is my only friend in the silence of night. A guy needs some comfort when he can't sleep, doesn't he?

The day grows dark and I am alone.
Alone. I wonder if I really am?

That word gets used so often, but does anyone stop to think and look around before they come to that conclusion? A lot of the time all we feel is the sensation of being alone. No one around us. No friends. No family. No one to talk to. We all feel like that sometimes, and sometimes it gets too much and so we find ourselves doing stupid things or hurting ourselves or others.

Friends aren't always the most reliable people, and to talk to your family about your troubles is only going to make them worry unnecessarily. You don't tell anyone that something is wrong, because then they will worry and "try to help," etc. They're "help" does more harm than good. It's hard to explain, but those that have been there understand without a doubt or question in mind. People tell you to smile and enjoy life. "Don't worry!" Stuff like that. It's ironic, because usually it's those same people who have hurt or upset you to begin with that are telling you this.

It's said that smiling makes you feel better, but in reality, a smile fixes nothing. All it does is show people what they want to see, and possibly make you forget your problems for a while; but soon enough they'll be back and the smile that you tried so hard to keep painted on is gone like a virgin on prom night.

I don't know what I'm trying to get across, or even if there is a point to what I am writing at all, but I guess that can be said for nearly everything. What is the world trying to get across to us? Is there a point to life? I think it's funny that I should ask those questions like this, because I am asking myself everyday, and everyday I ask myself, I give myself the same answer. Sometimes "Yes," most the time "No." Even when I could be laughing hard and enjoying life, in the back of my mind I'm still questioning life, asking myself if there's reason for me to go on. The depression is always there. Thoughts of suicide flood my mind nearly everyday, but I know it isn't worth it. My sisters shouldn't have to live with that on top of everything else they go through, so for their sakes I keep myself breathing. I guess I give a shit about others, afterall.

I ask myself why I give a shit sometimes. Sometimes I ask it a few times a day, though I guess most people would ask themselves, too. Whether the answer I've come to is a reason or an excuse for myself, I don't know, but this is my conclusion as to why. My father is a selfish, arrogant, abusive asshole who maybe doesn't really give a shit (only pretends to) until his own personal needs are met; and because of this, I don't want to turn out like him. I've decided to try and care about others' needs first. I know what it is to live without, and it sucks, but I have no problem in doing so if it means someone close to me is going to be a little better off. It's a bit of a catch-22 situation: I feel like shit because I barely have the money, food, or clothing I have to make it through the day myself, but if I don't give to someone who asks from me, I feel worse because I don't want to come across as selfish and turn out like the "Self-Righteous One", so I'll go without. I think this over and wonder if it's the right thing to do, and I still don't have an answer, but I'll try to keep doing so until the right answer is given.

THE DESPONDENT:
Part Three

The Poetry

*We have to be reminded constantly
that there is light and warmth after
all the darkness.
It's in the darkness we start to
feel safe in isolation.*

This is dangerous.

*Part Three speaks of hope.
Life.
Belief in a new world.
The REAL truth.*

The experiences depicted in these are real.

*I now feel and believe these to be true
in complete explicit detail.*

Tomorrow

Tomorrow is a new start.
Let's heal your broken heart.
Leave the pain of yesterday.
Yes, some memories will remain.

Tomorrow, the sun will rise again.
Don't let the fear of the unknown settle in.
Bitterness will only hurt you.
Your future lies ahead.

Do you wanna give your heart
One more try?
Or are you gonna waste your love
In heartbreak lies?
Can you learn to breathe again?
Will you let the sunshine in?

Do you wanna give your heart
One more try?
Or are you gonna waste your love
In heartbreak lies?
Will you let the sunshine in?
Can you learn to love again?

Tomorrow is a new start.
Tomorrow, the sun will rise again.
Will you learn to love again?
Your future lies ahead.

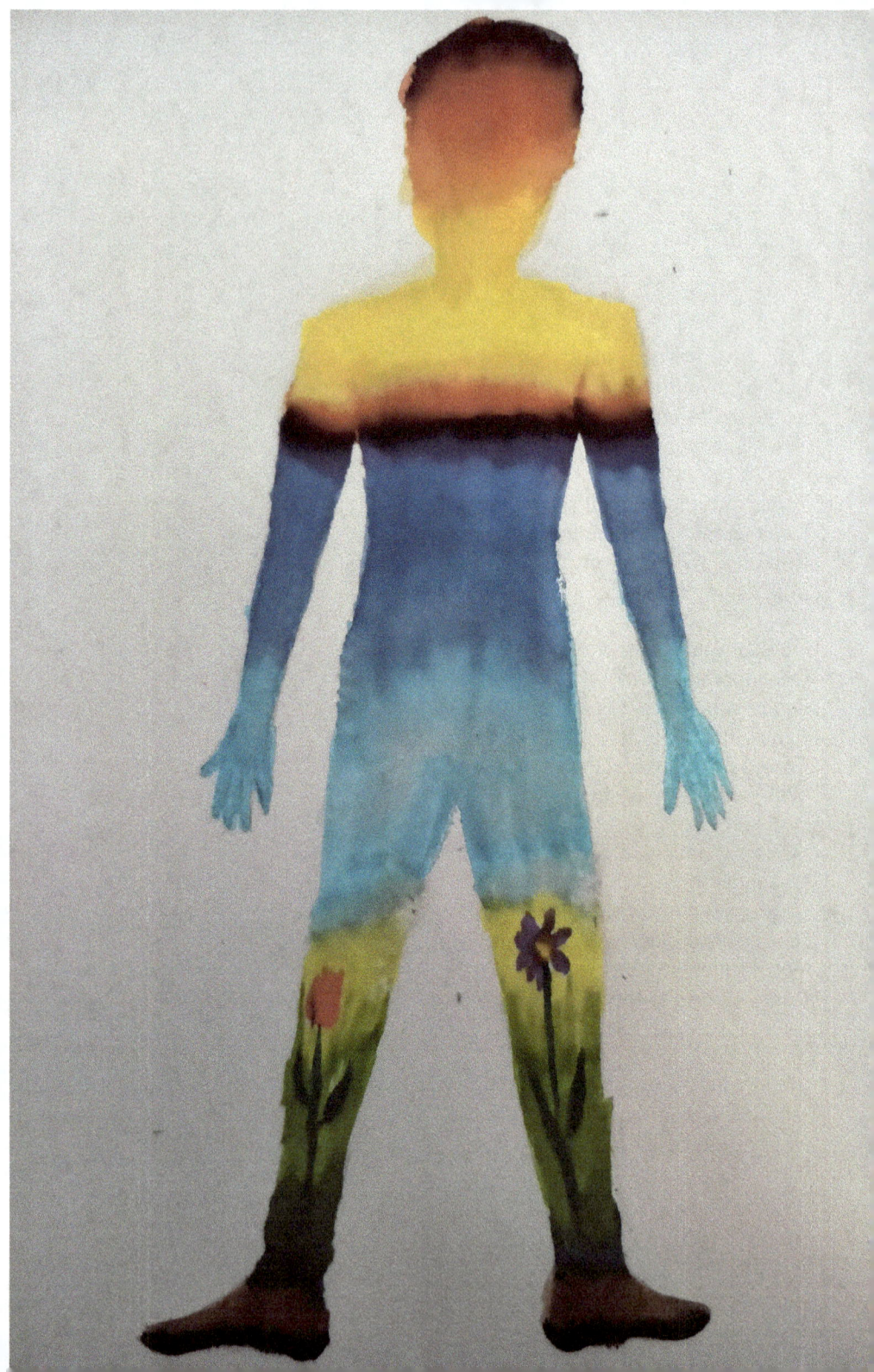

Eastbound

Are you afraid of the dark, young one?
Are you going to hide from the moon?
How can I, Mister?

Why gossip about yesterday, young mum?
The father may be gone, but look at your son.
He can count to four on his toes now.

Why hate on the bitch who took your house, young man?
Your daughter worships the ground you walk on.

Some questions matter
Some things are best left unsaid
Cliche or not
What you think determines where you make your bed

Stand tall, young one
And though your demons may lurk in the shadows
Turn around and watch for the rising sun
It's always darkest before the dawn

Put down the knife, young one
The man who raped you was killed by a car this morning
Untie the noose, young one
Your unborn child will change the world

Now face east
Let yourself be heard
Moving forward, step by step

Let the sun quiver with fear
You are strong

Why Worry?

Does the bird know it's haven before nightfall?
Does the tree know if it will grow or be made a chair?
Does the Mother know what she is doing one day to the next with her newborn?
Do aliens really exist?

Some questions matter,
And some quite not.
Regardless of the answer you provide,
Tomorrow is still going to happen.

Are you afraid of the dark?
Does that mean you will hide from the moon?

Demons may lurk in the shadows
Turn around
Face East
Light will come again

Why be concerned about things that are not yours to control?

Take A Step Back

Take a step back,
Learn how to breathe.
Take a step back
And be.

Observe in silence.
Take things in.
Despite what goes on,
Trust what's within.

Taking Control

Is this a storm I can feel building?
I can feel the clouds thicken
I'm hanging on to these last rays of sun -
Hoping, Praying:

    "Please don't rain. Not today!
    Things are finally going right"

Alas! My boat is drifting further from the shore
The winds have quickened.
The waves!
They're forming more powerful

              BE STILL!

For the first time in my life
I'm holding on to the last
Of the suns rays of light.

In The Silence

Dancing on the flames of life
Stirring up the wind
Singing with cicada wings
The cool of the night engulfs

Footprints in the cold damp sand
Waves softly lapping the shore
The sea breeze refreshes all
The moon smiles on

When there is nothing
When no one is around
The Spirits of our Earth are near
Listen to their Secrets

...And When Does Our Journey Begin?

Hours today were spent at the beach
This morning my spirits were naught but bleak
It's amazing how empowered the waves on the sand
Can make you feel when times are bad

I walked and I smiled
Children played in the sun
Not a care in the world -
Their lives not yet begun

How powerful, How promising,
How beautifully charmed
How pleasant our lives quite are
When spent in the sun

Writing these anotations I've come to realise
The flow of my rhymes -
As waves, they could be described
Although familiar, and today very calm;
Each set is different,
Unique,
In Psalm

Wisdoms Woods

For every time I've failed,
For every time I've screwed up,
For every time I've said "I'm Sorry,"
And for every time I've not.

For every heart I've broken,
For every stone unturned,
For every one I've damaged
Due to an action or spoken word.

No, I'm not a loser.
I know I am no failure.
Some things take longer to learn.
In the end, I'll have things mastered.

Regret? I've had aplenty.
Self-loathing? I've lived that, too.
Walked away too many times,
Stepping closer to something new.

I know where I'm going.
I'm taking longer than I should,
But these setbacks are not failures,
Only detours through Wisdoms Woods.

THE DESPONDENT
Part Four

The Final Chapter

Behaviours are learned very quickly from a young age, and are very hard to break once they're learned. You can beat such behaviours and change your life around. It takes a lot of different things, but as the old saying goes, *A journey of a thousand miles begins with a single step.*

And a journey of a thousand miles is one I've lived, no doubt about it. I hate when people ask me where I'm from, because I don't know how to answer. Where was I living before where I am now, or where was I born? What was my family like? People may wonder at times why I've been so unstable or closed off with a lot of things. I think the following could explain some of it, and, I hope, that the summary of my life which follows may provide further insight and understanding to you, the reader, of how different situations or family affairs, could negatively impact someone for a great chunk of their life, even if it is seemingly small or insignificant.

By the time I was twenty-one, I had permanently and temporarily lived in over 30 places, and by the time I had hit thirty, that number had increased by another 20+ places of accommodation.

Things were rarely good for me growing up in a house full of younger girls and no brothers. Everything had always come back to being my fault, getting in trouble for seemingly everything...

When I was nine years old, I tried running away from home. That's how old I was when I first knew I didn't like my dad, or that maybe things could be better in a place that wasn't at home. He has always been a heavy weight. My arse often with red marks for a while after what he called "a light tap", which was usually followed by the instruction of "stop crying before I give you something to cry about". He caught me on my way out the front door, told me he'd call the police on me if I ran away. At nine, I didn't realise I should have challenged his threat. Maybe life could have been a bit more pleasant growing up.

  A year or so later when I was ten, he threw me off my chair, spilling my dinner all over the floor and rubbed my face in it, telling me how ungrateful I was and then said that I had to pick it up off the floor and not leave the table until I had finished all of it. It was chicken and rice. That event came about because I was going through a period I didn't eat chicken, and was being a stubborn kid. Now, as an adult, I know I was being ungrateful – I mean, we were barely scraping by. My grandparents were sending us food, the local church was helping us out (all of this unknown to us kids, and no, that should not have made a difference to my attitude and demeanor); but that doesn't excuse his behaviour, nor does it remove the trauma and fear it birthed in me which I carry even now to this day. I struggle with anxiety and sometimes shut down or become angry especially when it comes to talking about something which may result in conflict, and quite often have issues with overbearing, loud individuals, especially if they happen to be in a position of authority and are throwing that around.

  During year eight, we were offered at school our year 9/10 electives. I wasn't doing too badly at school. Granted, I wasn't anywhere near the top of my classes, but I was somewhat enjoying it, and I wasn't failing. After going through my options, weighing them up with my interests, I eventually told my parents I wanted to study Physics and Marine Biology. They were my two chosen electives. Apparently, according to my parents at the time, they would likely be a bit difficult for me, and I should probably focus on something a bit simpler, more suited for my level. That single conversation instilled in my mind that I'm not going to be good at much, to not try even when things get difficult because there's always an easier option.

Anyway, I didn't like their decision, and I recall putting in those electives anyway. As with everything that happened in my life, my parents found out. I swear they must have had super secret government spy equipment or something, because nothing ever got past them. Around this time, we had also started going to a church a little shy of an hour north of where we lived. A few of the kids and teens there were homeschooling. Now, homeschooling was something I had heard my parents say was never going to be a thing they would ever do. After year eight finished, we packed house, moved almost an hour north of where we were living so it'd be easier to get to church, and started homeschooling... For two years! Why didn't we find a church closer? Well, fun little story – I'll give you the version I was told: My dad thought he knew better than all the other pastors in all the other suitable churches between where we lived and that one, constantly getting into arguments with them, and we either got kicked from them, or he decided they were bad churches for us. Whatever... but that's the in and out of why we were going to a church so far away..

When I was fifteen, year ten, still being homeschooled, my parents separated. The night my mother left, he and I got into an argument and sent me to my room. I dutifully, angrily, followed his instruction, then left the house. I could have gone to my friends' house, but I didn't. I don't know why. I ran to where I hoped my mother was, at the other end of town. Surprisingly, I was correct. A couple of hours later, she phoned him, asking if he knew where I was. He said I was in my room. He had no clue. Made me feel like he cared so much, that did. He hadn't bothered checking on me once. Mum never went home after that night, except to grab her things and leave her wedding ring the next day. A Sunday, while we were at church. And I think that's when she and I started having problems. I started blaming her, angry at her for not letting me go with her, not letting me know she was leaving. I didn't properly speak to her for months.

As I said earlier, everything while I was growing up seemed to have been my fault, or the result of something I had said or done... but after mum left, it seemed to get worse. There were always arguments to be had in the family growing up, always being isolated from my sisters not being allowed to mingle with them because they're girls – *"Leave them alone, Aaron!"* - and when there was yelling, there was trouble. Get sent off to my room, not to play elsewhere, see anyone, nada. As I mentioned before, we moved around a lot as well. As an adult now, I can't stand arguments, confrontation, conflict. For the longest of times, if I instigated something, I became angry, then redirected that anger at myself and closed up, often hurting people one way or another in the process. If I was on the receiving end, I either didn't back down and made an ass of myself, or I closed up and tried to leave the room, building, relationship, regardless if the person delivering was doing so from a hurt, upset, angry, constructive, viewpoint. If someone came at me with a raised voice or anger, in a *fight or flight* world, I generally took flight and only fought if flight was refused or blocked. Neither option helped, but it's all I knew. It's what I had observed for over fifteen years. It's what I learned for over fifteen years. Suffice it to say, my people skills weren't the greatest for the first thirty years of my life. Yes, they have only really started to develop, because only in recent years have I properly become aware and started taking ownership and attempting to cease living in the past and letting it affect me when certain events raise their heads. It's still difficult, but every step counts towards something. I'm now wearing blame and guilt for things that aren't my fault – like if someone doesn't reply to me for a few hours, I'll get anxious and upset because I might have said something which upset them. It's all really unreasonable and stupid, but knowing where it's coming from, it helps be able to silence that anxiety when I finally recognise it.

When I was sixteen, I learned firsthand about scams. I moved out west, first time living on my own away from any parents or adult guardians, because there was a church pastor out there offering an aviation course which combined itself with a counselling course. This sounded like a brilliant opportunity. I decided to go, and so we packed up the van and trailer with my stuff and I moved. A few months later, I phoned my dad to let him know that it was basically a sham, that I wasn't happy out there. I had made some friends though, and one of them lived down in Victoria. I was planning on moving back there with him to start a new life.

That wasn't allowed. I was to move back home and finish school, as I didn't complete year 10 while I was being homeschooled the year before.

Begrudgingly, reluctantly, I complied... but being back at home after living on my own for four months caused more issues than ever before, and for my third attempt and second success, I ran away from home. Off to mum again. I completed year 10 under her roof. I don't like to think about what I'd have done or become if my parents didn't separate or if I stayed under his roof. She has really been a lifesaver at times. (THANKS, MUM!)

After the school year ended, my father moved himself and my sisters 1200km north of me and my mother. This was tough. I didn't really see or speak to them as it was, but this removed the ability to be able to do so ever. In this town, I was struggling to find a job, so about three or four months into the next year, I moved up north and crashed on my dads couch for a couple of months while I looked for a job and a place to stay of my own. I eventually found both, and I was happy. It was in this house I turned eighteen, for those of you keeping track of a timeline.

However, as they say, all good things must come to an end, and I believe it. The start of the next year, my flatmate announced he was moving interstate. I decided to quit my job, and move back down south with Mum. There was no way I was crashing on dad's couch again, and time was running out for me to find somewhere to live myself as I was unable to take over the lease where I was.

It was while I was living with mum here that I started becoming angry, depressed, and quite unpleasant. It was here that I started visiting memories of how messed up things were with dad, what he had done, the family breakdown.... everything. Things in my head were not adding up, were not going right, and I started losing my foothold and slip downhill.

Between the age of 18 and 22 (some things are a little out of order, but I can tell you during this time), I was:
- homeless,
- acquired and lost various jobs,
- been cheated on,
- was raped,
- started smoking, and got into a life of drugs and alcoholism and partying,
- lived in a drafty caravan in the middle of Winter where the temperatures overnight often dropped near and below zero degrees centigrade,
- and lost many friends, one of whom I had been close with since I was 12 (miss you man, wherever you are).

Then, a short while after my 22nd birthday, I had a friend kill herself. Nothing can prepare you for something like that. I had not lost anyone before, and it shakes you up really badly.

During those crazy years, I began writing poetry as a way to deal with the hurt and pain – much healthier than some other options, but still... I couldn't avoid the inner turmoil and one day I broke completely and tried to take my own life. I have a particular ex-girlfriend to thank for pulling me out of the shower, a drunken, incoherent mess.

A year later, my mum, stepdad, and baby sister had already moved away north to be nearer the rest of my sisters, and I had finally had enough of life down south with nothing but a feeling of nothing left, especially prospects of a future. I had already made an attempt on my own life as it was. Sure, I had people and friends around me, but I couldn't cope anymore where I was. I had to get out.

I'd like to say that since then, life has been nothing but peachy, but as I should have known by now - moving away doesn't solve problems. Your issues are internal and need to be dealt with properly at some point. Although, yes, some towns are like poison or don't suit your personality and interest, or are not where you need or want to be and you do need to leave for your own sanity!

Between 21 and 31, and again, the timeline is messy in my head, so another list. I've been:
- in debt;
- diagnosed with Major Depression Disorder;
- my friend killed herself, as I previously mentioned;
- Mum battling her own mental health issues which resulted in suicide attempts;
- I've become a dad (see, not everything in my life has been bad!);
- more broken relationships;
- I've been prevented from seeing my son for long

periods of time on multiple occasions; and,
- I have a child I've never been allowed to meet

Some things have been handled well. Some things have not.

One thing I've learned in life is EVERYTHING either starts with or stops at you. Sure, you could be left in situations that aren't favourable because of someone elses actions and decisions; however, it stops at you. The choices you make every day, regardless of what happens, could determine the rest of your entire life. I think my story is a testament to that. It is far from an easy journey. I still have days that I struggle with. I still make poor decisions and react badly to situations at times.

At the start of the book I told you a vital truth:

THERE ARE NO QUICK FIXES.

I also told you another vital truth:

YOU ARE NOT ALONE.

No matter what it is you're going through, someone else has probably gone through it before. Reach out. Someone will see you. Someone will hear you – not only the words you are saying, but hear you with full comprehension because they may have been there themselves not too long ago. You never know the baggage and history someone carries with them, that they might be the ones who can help you with yours because they truly understand the struggle.

One thing which helped me turn my life around was an audio book my friend and mentor gave me, and a few years later, I went out and bought the paperback. (Something about turning pages myself and the smell ... You don't get that with audio books). Anyway, that particular book started me thinking and paying attention to things I haven't been doing as well as I could be, and opened my eyes to a few things. That book is called *The Slight Edge*, by Jeff Olson. A few other books which have really helped me, and may or may not help those of you struggling are *The 7 Habits of Highly Effective People* by Stephen R Covey, and *Developing the Leader Within You*, by John C Maxwell. Reading these three books, as well as spending a lot of time at the beach and in the bush away from people and drama, allowing myself to slow down and gather my thoughts really made a difference. Talking to people about what I was going through also made a huge difference. It didn't happen quickly. It didn't happen easily. As I said before, I still struggle, but the difference? I'm aware of it, pull myself up, and do my utmost to get on with it.

Being honest with others about what you've been through helps you become honest with yourself. Helps you take ownership of some things, and creates some level of clarity and closure. Find someone you trust, or find a stranger, and maybe drop a hint of it in passing, in general conversation, as a whisper or as a shout. The more you mention something in passing, the easier it becomes to talk about as a serious thing. It doesn't make past actions right, but it makes future mindsets and behaviours simpler; and helps others better understand you and your past and current behaviours and actions as well. It really does help to talk about things. Nothing should be considered taboo. Nothing should be considered untouchable. The only way to find someone who cares enough to listen to your struggles is by opening up and talking about them.

Otherwise, no one will know you're hurting, and you'll
continue to think that no one cares about you.
This is a fact and that is a lie.

The world almost lost me because of it.
The world almost lost Mum because of it.
The world lost Aleysha because of it.

SOME FINAL THOUGHTS

I said at the start of this that behaviours are learned - but let me expand that to our attitudes, our responses, our actions and reactions, and other general thought patterns. Mums and Dads, we need to be so careful with not just what we say to and around our children, but <u>HOW</u> we say things, too. Even if it's just a bit of tongue-in-cheek, or to keep them on their toes while they're young - if our children aren't made aware these things are not reflective of our actual feelings or thoughts towards them, or that they maybe feel insecure or upset by them without our knowing (and we know that kids are great at hiding and lying about their emotions and wants at times), it can affect them in years to come, maybe not even until adulthood.

I remember being told if something was too difficult to put it in the "too-hard basket and move on". I'm sure the context must have been lost on me when I was younger because that thought pattern carried onto general life over time. *Oh, something is too hard, move on. Oh, this is difficult. Move on.* And being told you're an idiot, not smart enough, or the classic *"you're not doing it right. Get out of the way, I'll do it"* (and not being shown how to actually do it and try it for myself so it's properly learned) - things such as these happen enough times, over time you start to believe you won't be able to achieve anything, be good enough to ever reach your dreams and ambitions - *Ha! Ambitions and dreams, what's the point? What even are they?* Even now when people tell me I'm smart and have the ability to do *something*, and I find it difficult to believe them, and bits and pieces of my past start to resurface to try and bring me down so that I cannot accept the compliment or praise just given me. I barely made it through high school. What could I offer the world? I'm not a qualified *anything*, just an average guy.

This.

This is what I can offer the world. Just an average guy trying to share his story to maybe help others who might be struggling with their depression and anxiety; so to those thoughts of uselessness, I say *"Shut up!"* (and I do this quite verbally. I swear some people might think I'm crazy if they heard me giving myself little pep-talks sometimes), because people do need to know they are not alone with these thoughts; that people do know what it's like to live every day and every night, barely getting a wink of sleep, carrying a feeling that you're less than nothing; and above all, people need to know that there are people out there who care about them and understand *(I know, "Don't tell me you understand, you don't know me, you don't know my story. Fuck you.")* how much it hurts and hardens you, separates you from your friends and family and hobbies, and well, everything.

I might be an average writer, with a financially poor background, mediocre education, and a history of gruelling depression which nearly landed me six feet under *(white boy problems, right?)* - but at the end of the day, I'm still here. Medication, opening up to friends and family, opening up to work colleagues... I couldn't have done it on my own. I know where "on my own" takes me, and is probably taking some of you. So if you're reading this and you're struggling or have connected with any of the themes raised in this book, speak up, speak out, ask for help. Similarly, if you aren't in this position, but know someone who is, take the time to let them know you're there... and be patient with them, love them. It's all that you need to do - the rest is up to them, us.

Acknowledgements And Thank-Yous:

To the reader: Thank you for your purchase and reading of "The Despondent". At time of writing, I am looking at different avenues to donate a portion of each sale to an Australian mental health awareness charity. Thank you for your support.

Those of my family who had a hand in raising me, for a lifetime of patience, encouragement, and guidance – especially with my early years of reading, which ultimately birthed my love for poetry and literature. There are FAR too many of you to name.

Special Thanks to:

Aunty Lynn for consistently encouraging me to put this together for years! I eventually folded and did so. Thank you so much. None of this would have happened without you!
My sister, **Renae Stone**, for providing illustrations for this book. I know I get a bit pushy and critical. Thanks for being awesome, putting up with me, and following through to the end.
Aunty Janet & My **Mum** – where and how do I start? You both have done so much for my love of literature!
Uncle Danny for your generous patience and support– all those talks did not fall on deaf ears. Thank you.
Mr Andrew Robertson, for your support and mentorship in so many areas. Thank you so much.

...And I really must thank those who helped me on the multiple occasions when I was homeless and/or struggling with my depression:
Shawn W, Michelle & David B, M.C., Danni H, Troy B, Jess B, Steve S, Aunty Lynn & Uncle Danny, Charlotte B, Aunty Chris & Uncle Dennis, H.M., Lauren O, Sarah R, Mum, Adam R, Tenille H, Matt P, and **so many others**.

THANK YOU

I might not be here today if it wasn't for some of you.

This book is dedicated to those we have lost to suicide.
May You Forever Rest In Peace.